D1518599

BROWN COMMUNITY COLLEGE

ROXY, MINNESOTA 22804

SERVICE LEARNING FOR TEENS™

WORKING FOR TOLERANCE AND SOCIAL CHANGE

THROUGH SERVICE LEARNING

NICKI PETER PETRIKOWSKI

ROSEN PUBLISHING®

New York

Published in 2015 by The Rosen Publishing Group, Inc.
29 East 21st Street, New York, NY 10010

Copyright © 2015 by The Rosen Publishing Group, Inc.

First Edition

All rights reserved. No part of this book may be reproduced in any form without permission in writing from the publisher, except by a reviewer.

Library of Congress Cataloging-in-Publication Data

Petrikowski, Nicki Peter.
Working for tolerance and social change through service learning/Nicki Peter Petrikowski.
        pages cm.—(Service learning for teens)
Includes bibliographical references and index.
ISBN 978-1-4777-7967-5 (library bound)
1. Service learning—United States—Juvenile literature. 2. Social change—United States—Juvenile literature. 3. Toleration—United States—Juvenile literature. I. Title.
LC220.5.P48 2015
361.3'70973—dc23

                                                    2014023247

Manufactured in the United States of America

CONTENTS

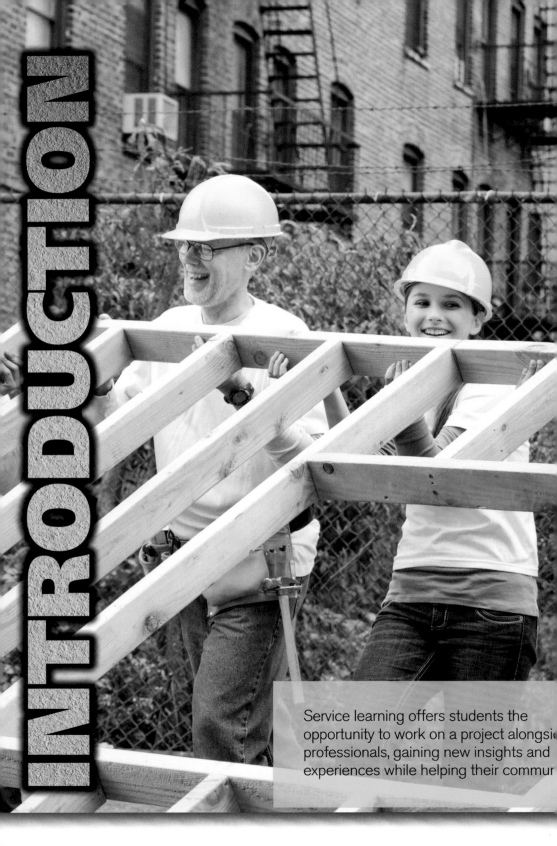

INTRODUCTION

Service learning offers students the opportunity to work on a project alongside professionals, gaining new insights and experiences while helping their community.

Service learning is a pedagogic model, or method of teaching. So shouldn't it be teachers rather than students who concern themselves with it? Looking at how widespread service learning has become in middle schools and high schools, as well as in higher education, over the course of the last three decades, teachers certainly are concerning themselves with it. However, it is worthwhile for students to acquaint themselves with service learning as well. Unlike other teaching methods, service learning does not simply count on the passive collaboration of students. Instead, it calls for their active involvement.

Service learning offers the chance for students to develop and introduce their own ideas. This sometimes means the opportunity to shape a project that a teacher has picked out, but it can also extend to creating the project itself. In addition, service learning addresses a complaint many students have about school. Students often grumble that it feels like the things they have to learn in school are far removed from any real-world application. Students wonder why they have to learn them at all. Happily, that does not apply to service learning, in which the service provided by the students has an impact on their community. In some cases, such as the projects aimed at causing social change through service learning that are the focus of this book, students have the opportunity to impact society as a whole. In a service-learning project, students get to make decisions that have actual comprehensible results and maybe even change the world. Besides, getting an insight into and some experience with how society operates outside of regular school life is more than a welcome side effect in regard to the exploration of possible future career options.

The definition of tolerance is "a willingness to accept feelings, habits, or beliefs that are different from your own." Tolerance is necessary for peaceful coexistence in a diverse society. However, it can be a big, somewhat abstract goal to work toward. Service-learning projects encourage students to set concrete objectives that help advance tolerance. The structured ways in which students reflect on what they learned from the projects that they participated in also makes service learning a useful tool for addressing big concepts like tolerance and intolerance.

CHAPTER ONE

EDUCATION FOR THE CIVIC-MINDED

There are countless definitions of what service learning is, ranging from simple explanations to those that seem overly complicated in their attempt to be as precise as possible. For example, the National Youth Leadership Council defines service learning on its website as "an approach to teaching and learning in which students use academic knowledge and skills to address genuine community needs." In her *Complete Guide to Service Learning*, Cathryn Berger Kaye goes into a little more detail and defines service learning as "a research-based teaching method where guided or classroom learning is applied through action that addresses an authentic community need in a process that allows for youth initiative and provides structured time for reflection on the service experience and demonstration of acquired skills and knowledge."

Both of these definitions address the duality present in the name itself: it is both learning through serving and being able to apply what has been learned while serving. To stress how closely related these two things are, people sometimes choose to hyphenate the name: service-learning.

The difference between service learning and more conventional forms of learning is obvious. One gives the opportunity to apply learned knowledge and skills in a practical manner. The other usually does not, instead focusing on the acquisition of theoretical knowledge.

Learning is, of course, an integral part of school life. However, many students wish for a more practical approach that connects the subject matter to real life.

The distinction between service learning and social service or volunteer work, which many schools offer or maybe even require, is not as blatant. While both should hopefully address genuine community needs rather than the service being an end in itself, it is not the stated aim of community service for the student to learn while engaged in it. Service learning, on the other hand, has the express goal of educating participants. The chances are good that students providing community service will learn something from it. However, the structured time for reflection mentioned by Kaye in her definition of service learning is what sets it apart. In fact, that reflection is what connects the service and the learning.

HOW TO START AND GET INVOLVED

A good service-learning project should invite student participation every step of the way. That may even mean that the impulse to start a service-learning project comes from a student, not the teacher, if the teacher is open to the idea. There are two prerequisites for service learning: It has to be linked to the curriculum (what is taught in class), and it has to address a community need. In most cases a teacher who intends to start a service-learning project will have chosen the subject matter accordingly, allowing the students to make the connection between, for example, a book they have read in class and problems in their community. It doesn't necessarily have to be planned like this, though. Sometimes a connection between the learning material and real life will just present itself without being planned in advance. Either way, a service-learning project starts with identifying the genuine community need that will be the focus of the project. Young people are members of their community just as much as adults are. They are as perceptive about community needs just as much

A school community includes the students who attend the school, as well as the teachers, administrators, and other staff members who work there.

if not more so. After all, young people see the world with fresh eyes, whereas older people may have gotten used to the way things are and have come to accept them without questioning.

Sometimes a genuine need will simply be obvious to those who have perceived it. Other times it might be useful to first consider what is meant by "community." Most commonly, "community" refers to a town or a neighborhood, the immediate area where you live. A service-learning project does not need to restrict itself to that particular meaning when identifying a community need, though. While it is certainly possible to deal with a need that is close to home, be it at your own school or in your general area, it is also an option to look at a larger community and address a need at the state, national, or even global level. Especially when dealing with problems of social injustice, there is hope that addressing problems at a higher level will result in positive changes in one's more immediate community as well.

AIMING FOR THE STARS?

It is important to set a goal that is reachable, though. It might be an illustrious endeavor to try to stamp out intolerance in the world, but regrettably that is not something a single service-learning project is likely to achieve. Similarly a goal that is as unspecific as "doing something for social justice at school/in your hometown," while narrowed down geographically, is unlikely to reach a satisfying outcome. The goal you set yourself for your project should be clear and precise so that you actually know when you have reached it. It should be challenging because when you want to make a difference and improve your community, it makes little sense to give less than your best. But there also needs to be a realistic chance that you will be able to accomplish it. Time has to be taken into consideration as well. Although it sometimes may seem that it is, a school year is not endless, and usually only a part of it will be devoted to service learning. Hence it is necessary to find a goal that can be accomplished in the time available.

With the world being as complex as it is, there is always the possibility that you might not be able to accomplish your goal no matter how good your intentions are and how well prepared you are. Things beyond your control can go wrong. People can prove unwilling to cooperate. These are possibilities that you have to accept. If there are setbacks, it is important not to get discouraged and simply give up. Reflect on what has gone wrong and why. See if you can find a way to reach your goal after all. Service learning shows students what it means and what it takes to be a valuable member of and a positive influence on their community. That includes not giving up on the idea of making things better.

THE HISTORY OF SERVICE LEARNING

The term "service learning" was coined in the 1960s, a time when service to one's country was in the spotlight in U.S. politics. This sentiment was most succinctly expressed by President John F. Kennedy in his inaugural address, in which he urged Americans, "Ask not what your country can do for you; ask what you can do for your country." To this end the Peace Corps was established under Kennedy in 1961. Volunteers In Service To America (VISTA), an anti-poverty program Kennedy had the idea for, was created under

This Peace Corps volunteer is teaching children in Nepal. Over the years, more than two hundred thousand Americans have served in the Peace Corps.

his successor, Lyndon B. Johnson, in 1965. It was in keeping with the spirit of the times when educators Robert Sigmon and William Ramsey established the Manpower Development Internship Program at the Southern Regional Education Board in Atlanta, Georgia, in 1967. Its goals included education as well as meeting genuine community needs. Sigmon and Ramsey called this "service learning." The term and the practice it describes quickly gained popularity.

 JOHN DEWEY

While there are many people and institutions that have influenced service learning as we know it today, American philosopher and educational reformer John Dewey (1859–1952) is generally seen as one of the most prominent forerunners of service learning. Dewey taught philosophy and psychology as a professor at the University of Michigan, the University of Chicago, and Columbia University. He was critical of unchecked capitalism, as he feared it would transfer power to the rich at the expense of ordinary people and ultimately threaten democracy. For Dewey, charity was not a viable option to deal with the problem of poverty because he understood charity to assume the existence of a superior class (those who give charity) and an inferior class (those who receive and possibly depend on charity). Instead he was a proponent of change in society that would make the community a better place for everybody. He identified education as the key to this transformation. He argued that it would give everybody the same opportunity to succeed and serve democracy as a whole by improving society in general.

Dewey understood knowledge as a tool we use to respond to and deal with our situation in the world. This made him a proponent of experiential education, arguing that people learn best from experience and reflecting on that experience. Knowledge sticks best if we have used it in a concrete, practical, and meaningful way, when we see that it helps us solve actual problems and accomplish something. That concept is at the core of service learning and, although Dewey never called it that, his theory offers support to this teaching method.

Dewey was also ahead of his time in regard to social change, as he called for inclusive learning environments at a time when students were still separated by class, race, and sex. He also believed that students should learn to solve problems together as a group rather than individually. This would prepare and encourage them to cooperate and contribute to the civic good when they entered the social world, making them valuable members of a democratic society.

In the 1980s, a number of organizations were founded that helped establish networks and turn service learning into a reform movement. These included the National Center for Service-Learning for Early Adolescents (founded in 1981), Campus Outreach Opportunity League (1984), National Campus Compact (1985), and Youth Service America (1986). These organizations led to several laws in support of service learning being

Teaching or tutoring younger children is one service students can provide during a service-learning project.

passed on a national level in the 1990s. The National and Community Service Act, signed by President George H. W. Bush in 1990, authorized grants for schools to support service learning. The National and Community Service Trust Act, signed by President Bill Clinton in 1993, created Learn and Serve America, the largest funder of service-learning programs in the United States. Learn and Serve America engaged more than a million participants (out of the estimated 4.7 million students from kindergarten to twelfth grade who take part in service-learning projects every year).

However, Congress eliminated funding for Learn and Serve America in 2011, forcing the states to find different ways of financing service-learning projects in their schools. While the loss of federal funding poses a challenge (and campaigning for funding for Learn and Serve America might make an interesting service-learning project itself) the popularity of this teaching method remains unbroken. While twenty-seven states mentioned service learning in state policy in the year 2000, twelve years later that number had increased to forty-two. Close to half of all public high schools in the United States offer some form of service learning. Hundreds of colleges offer academic credit for service learning. While a survey found that only 37 percent of Americans were familiar with the

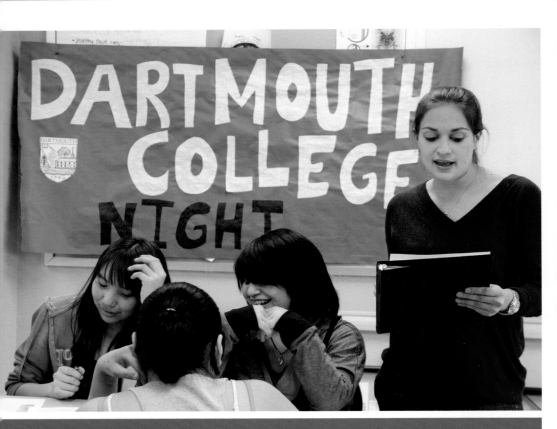

Many colleges offer opportunities for service learning. One example is the Alternative Spring Break program, which lets students give back to their communities rather than go on vacation during their break.

term "service learning," 90 percent were in support of it when the idea behind service learning was explained to them. This teaching method is not only popular in its place of origin, either. It has spread and is popular in Canada, Europe, and other places the world over for showing students how to get involved and make a positive change in their communities.

CHAPTER TWO

SERVICE LEARNING IN ACTION

After the decision has been made to start a service-learning project, and a genuine community need has been identified that the participants' service is meant to address, it is time to formulate a plan for how to address it.

POSSIBLE WAYS TO SERVE

While there are many different kinds of service that can be provided as part of a service-learning project, Cathryn Berger Kaye names four different categories of service: direct service, indirect service, advocacy, and research.

When participants are interacting directly with the people for whom they are providing a service, it is direct service. Examples of this might include tutoring younger children or teaching senior citizens how to navigate the Internet.

Those who are providing indirect service are not in direct, face-to-face contact with the recipients of their service. This may be the case when collecting food or clothes for those in need, which may not be

Collecting donations for those in need, be it clothes, food, or money, is a common way for schools to engage their students in helping the community.

handed out by the participants themselves but given to a homeless shelter or a similar facility. Projects that do not serve a readily identifiable group of recipients and instead benefit the community as a whole or the environment also fall into this category. Examples of this include cleaning the neighborhood or creating a mural to beautify it.

Advocacy means supporting a cause by raising awareness of the issue and hopefully getting others involved. Examples might include producing information brochures or writing letters to politicians, like the mayor of your town or your state's governor.

Research projects give the participants the opportunity to test their theoretical knowledge in the field. For example, a service-learning project in biology class might observe the distribution of an endangered species in the area, or a social studies class could develop a survey on how socially just citizens of its hometown consider their community to be. The results of these studies can be passed on to the appropriate authority. They can also be the starting point for another service-learning project.

Keith Morton, in his article "The Irony of Service," uses three categories of service. "Charity" means the meeting of a need in the short term. "Project" means something that lasts longer (like tutoring or building houses) and is often done in cooperation with other organizations. "Social change" aims to address the root causes of problems in society and probably involves advocacy. These form a hierarchy of sorts, as these categories are tiered by how deep an impact they are likely to have. All forms of service can be meaningful, though.

In regard to tolerance and social change, some of these categories of service seem more fitting than others. While you can give a hungry person something to eat and thus satisfy his or her need at least for a time, it is not possible to solve the problem of somebody who is facing prejudice, intolerance, and injustice in the same straightforward way. You can and should, of course, treat people with respect and tolerance. That does not compensate for the lack thereof they get from others or maybe even society as a whole. To address such a social evil, you have to direct your service toward advocacy to beget social change.

HE WHO FAILS TO PLAN, PLANS TO FAIL

Once you are clear on which way you can address the community need you have chosen, you need to investigate it further and prepare. When gathering information about a community need, collecting what you have experienced or observed yourself is a good starting point. It helps to set out what you have collected in writing. Of course this will garner more results when the subject of the service-learning project is a local need, with which participants will have more firsthand experience than with nationwide or global needs. It is worth remembering, though, that personal experience can be deceiving in that it will differ from person to person. No one person's experience is universal. Just because one person has never faced prejudice or discrimination does not mean those things do not exist. The experience of somebody who has had the misfortune to encounter them a lot is not necessarily representative either. Therefore you need to consult other sources beyond personal experience. These may be the experiences of other members of the community that can be collected through interviews or surveys. You can also do research by reading books on the subject, looking up statistics on the Internet, and keeping an eye open for coverage of your chosen subject in newspapers, on the radio, or on TV. All of this will help you get a clearer picture of what you are dealing with.

The community need is not the only thing you need to investigate, though. You also need to look at yourself and how you are equipped to deal with the problem you are facing. People don't always have a clear idea of what they are good at, be it that they

Preparation is the key to a successful service-learning project. You need to set your goals and have a clear plan on how to reach them.

are too modest or overconfident. Therefore, it can help to partner up and interview each other about your skills and talents. Also discuss how these might prove valuable for reaching your goal. Keeping a list

> ## SERVICE LEARNING AND CAREER EXPLORATION

Service-learning projects often offer the opportunity to meet members of the community from various backgrounds. As students cooperate with these community members, they will learn about their jobs, giving the students an insight into possible career options.

Who students will interact with depends on the nature of the project, of course. Employees of government agencies or nonprofit organizations that are concerned with the same community need that the service learning project is addressing are likely to make an appearance. Journalists often take an interest in students' endeavors. Local businesses are usually good cooperation partners when it comes to funding projects that benefit the community. When it comes to building things, professional craftsmen are called into action. Seeing these people at work and possibly working alongside them gives students the opportunity to learn more about their own interests and strengths. This may give the students an idea about what career they want to pursue (or at least about what career is not for them). Having some hands-on experience in your chosen field during the process of serving never hurts.

of skills and talents represented in your group may be worthwhile so that you can assign roles based on who is most qualified to fill them. It is equally as valuable to know what you can't do as well as what you can. Only when you realize that you aren't good at something can you prepare accordingly and either learn what you need to know or recruit the help of somebody who can do what you cannot.

Along with a list of skills you have at your disposal (or that you may need to learn or recruit), you will also need a list of the resources needed to bring your plans to fruition. Learning materials may be available at your school. Additional books, and possibly newspapers, can be found at the local library. What you will need beyond that will depend on the project in question, of course. If you want to clean up the neighborhood, you need some brooms and trash bags. If you want to build something, you need access to tools. If you want to produce informative literature, you need the proper software. While students can likely find a lot of what they need at home, that might not always be the case.

What do you do when you have to buy something for your service-learning project? Maybe the school has a budget for that, maybe not. You might have to raise money to cover your expenses. Holding a bake sale or car wash can easily cover relatively small sums. The project participants may also choose to do without luxuries like going to the movies for a set amount of time and contribute their own money to show solidarity for their cause. When it comes to larger amounts of money, you will have to explore the possibilities for

If your service-learning project needs money, there is a good chance you may have to raise it yourself. A car wash is one of the time-tested methods to do that.

funding through other channels. Maybe the state has a program that offers grants for service-learning projects. There could be nonprofit organizations or foundations you can cooperate with. If you can show them how your project will benefit the community, you might be able to convince local businesses to contribute. It certainly is possible for young people to raise the funds for big projects. This was proved by the Youth Dreamers

(www.youthdreamers.org), which started out as a group
of middle school students at Stadium School in Balti-
more and went on to fulfill their dream. They addressed
a need they had seen in their community, which lacked
a place where organized activities for adolescents could
take place after school. Since the project started in
2001, they have raised more than $900,000. This was
enough to buy and renovate an abandoned home to
turn it into a youth center, named the Dream House.

ACTION AND REFLECTION

When all of the prep work is done, it is time to put
your plan into action and use your skills and knowledge to benefit the community. During the action
phase, there should be time set aside for reflection,
which forms the connection between service and
learning. Cathryn Berger Kaye calls it "a pause button
that gives students the time to explore the impact of
what they are learning and its effect on their thoughts
and future actions." Often this is done via group dis-
cussion or Q and A sessions, but reflection does not
always take the form of talking about what you have
seen and done. It is also possible to keep a journal
or write about your service experience in another way
(poems, essays, etc.), which often helps in formulating
your thoughts more clearly. Sometimes role-playing
exercises, skits, or charades can be helpful.

Not every participant in a service-learning project is fond of these pauses, though. To some it may
seem that the periods of time set aside for reflection
take away time from actively pursuing the goal that

Taking the time to think about and discuss the progress of your service-learning project is just as much a part of it as the work you are doing to benefit the community.

was set for the project. Why sit around and reflect when there is still so much to be done to help and improve the community? As has been mentioned, the pauses for reflection exist to help participants learn. Aside from processing their service intellectually, the pauses may also help participants deal with what they have experienced emotionally. Being confronted with things like poverty, hunger, prejudice, discrimination, and so on can be difficult, especially since most youths who are not directly affected by these are usually sheltered from them. It can be demanding to stand up for social justice.

Taking the time to reflect on their service does not only benefit those who are providing it, though. Thinking about their experiences will make it clear to them what has gone right and what has gone wrong, where their plan worked and where they will have to try something different moving forward. Mistakes can be analyzed and, hopefully, that will prevent them from being made again in the future. Unforeseen problems and demands can be addressed and the plan adjusted accordingly. This means that this "downtime" is anything but and that it has a beneficiary effect not only for the participants of the service-learning project but also for the community.

Putting your thoughts about your service-learning experience in writing helps formulate them more clearly. Sharing them with others can help you deal with that experience intellectually and emotionally.

CROSSING THE FINISH LINE

Every service-learning project has to come to an end at some point, hopefully after it has reached its intended goal and fulfilled the plan to benefit the community. That is a reason to celebrate, but not by throwing yourself a party and patting yourself on the back for a job well done. After all, the goal is to contribute to society and address a genuine need, not to gain some kind of reward. A more fitting way to bring such an altruistic endeavor to a close is by presenting the results of the service to a broader public. Through displays, presentations, and per-formances, participants can show what they have learned from their experience and what they have accomplished. This gives them the opportunity to reflect on it themselves one more time and to give others a chance to appreciate (and be inspired by) their contribution to society.

CHAPTER THREE

SOCIAL CHANGE: FROM SOCIETY TO THE CLASSROOM

Social change is an extremely broad term, encompassing all alterations in how a society works. Societies are changing constantly as value systems and behavior patterns shift.

On a small scale you can observe the effects of social change by looking at your parents or grandparents. They often will have difficulties accepting things the younger generation perceives as perfectly normal, as they grew up in a different time and were taught different values. Although these changes in what is perceived as acceptable are usually fairly small in the grand scheme of things, they are often a cause for conflict between children and their elders.

Social change can come about as a consequence of outside factors. For example a change in the environment can force a society to adapt to new conditions. Contact with other societies will have an effect when people see what others do differently, and possibly better, and incorporate this newly acquired knowledge into their lives. Developments from within the society

Women fighting for their right to vote is one example of social change being brought about by a group of people standing up to make society more just.

itself can have an impact as well, such as technological or medical breakthroughs. Social change can also be actively pursued through ideological and political movements.

> THE CIVIL RIGHTS MOVEMENT

One famous example of a movement that brought about social change in U.S. history is the civil rights movement. This mass protest movement fought—nonviolently—for civil rights for black Americans. After the Civil War, slaves had been emancipated and granted basic civil rights. However, they continued to face oppression through racial segregation, disenfranchisement, and acts of violence, especially in the South. This resulted in a long struggle that reached its climax and finally its resolution in the 1950s and 1960s.

After Rosa Parks was famously arrested for refusing to give up her seat on a bus in Montgomery, Alabama, to a white passenger on December 1, 1955, the black community boycotted the Montgomery bus system for a year until it was desegregated. One of the leaders of the boycott was Martin Luther King Jr., who subsequently became the most important leader of the civil rights movement. His "I Have a Dream" speech, given on August 28, 1963, when more than two hundred thousand people marched on Washington, D.C., to demonstrate for civil and economic rights for African Americans, is one of the most famous speeches in history. A year later he was awarded the Nobel Peace Prize for his nonviolent resistance against racial discrimination. King was assassinated on April 4, 1968.

While King and the civil rights movement brought about many positive changes, they did not wipe out all racism in the United States. Social change can clearly be a long and painful process.

The changes a society undergoes can be slow and come about almost imperceptibly for the individual. They can also be so drastic that they turn society upside down, sometimes practically overnight. The most drastic changes are commonly referred to as "revolutions." "Revolution" does not necessarily mean a violent outburst. During the Neolithic Revolution, approximately ten thousand years ago, many human cultures left behind their nomadic lifestyle as hunter-gatherers in favor of settling down, domesticating animals, and planting seeds, a social change necessary for our current society's existence. The same is true for the Industrial Revolution in the eighteenth and nineteenth centuries and the Digital Revolution that started in the second half of the twentieth century. Most people don't even want to consider what life would be like without computers, cell phones, and the Internet, which have brought societies around the world closer together than ever before. Other revolutions take the form of political upheaval and war, like the American Revolution and the French Revolution.

Which form social change takes depends on many factors, not least how pressing the need for change is and how many people are affected by it. At some

The Digital Revolution has brought about tremendous social change. Not too long ago, having the whole world at your fingertips anywhere you go, as we do now thanks to portable computers and wireless Internet technology, was unthinkable.

point masses of downtrodden and starving peasants will probably stop trying to bring about social change by petitioning their feudal masters and explore other means, whereas people living in a free and wealthy democratic society are unlikely to consider guillotining aristocrats a necessary or desirable option. But even a democratic society is not always as democratic as it could be, nor is it always free of prejudice and injustice. That is where service learning can step in.

SERVICE LEARNING FOR SOCIAL CHANGE

While social change has a very broad definition, in the context of service learning it is most often related to the question of intolerance and injustice.

The goal of a service-learning project is to address a community need, and many communities are in need of more tolerance and justice in regard to skin color, religion, gender, sexual orientation, physical ability, age, and so forth.

Some schools and teachers shy away from these topics, as they are deemed political, but as Susan Benigni Cipolle points out in *Service-Learning and Social*

Physically disabled people often find that a lack of social justice puts very real barriers in their paths. Making sure your school is accessible is one possible service-learning project.

Justice, "Education in general and all service-learning programs in particular are political in that they either support the status quo or work to change it." By not actively trying to bring about social change, you are upholding the way things are, including any injustices and inequalities you perceive in your community.

That may seem daunting, impossible even. How are students supposed to change the world for the better when the adults who have more influence on society don't seem able to make it fair and free for all to live in? The pursuit of equality and justice is an ongoing process, not something that could realistically be brought about in one fell swoop. Every little bit that contributes to that process is valuable. It is not unusual for young people to feel disengaged or even angry because they think they are powerless, but a successful service-learning project that addresses a community need can change that outlook.

CONNECTING SOCIAL CHANGE TO THE CURRICULUM

Service learning can be used in every school subject. Although some others lend themselves more easily to the topic of social change, even seemingly unlikely candidates like science and physical education offer points of contact. Many service-learning projects benefit from an interdisciplinary approach.

Social studies is concerned with how society works, so finding links to the topics of tolerance and social change should be easy. From discussing current political decisions and their effects on your community to learning about human rights and how they are upheld (or not) in different parts of the world, social studies offers many opportunities for starting service-learning projects and getting involved.

The same is true for history, a subject that in large part covers how society used to work and how it has changed. Learning about the women's suffrage movement in class is a good starting point for thinking about women's rights today, for example. When studying the settlement of the United States, you could take the opportunity to examine and draw attention to its ramifications for Native Americans.

Literature and language classes offer connections to the subject of social justice through works of fiction, such as George Orwell's *Animal Farm*. Biographies of people who have experienced intolerance or who have worked for social change are another good entry point. Looking at how language works is a good starting point as well. Words influence the way we think about and perceive the world; they can manipulate, sugarcoat, or condemn. It can be enlightening to closely examine the vocabulary that news reports, editorials, and the speeches of politicians use to discuss issues of social justice.

When analyzing statistics in math class, you can look at material that is relevant to social justice. You can even create your own surveys. You might also calculate the benefits of a fund-raising endeavor and measure them against the costs, determining how effective it was and how it could have been more effective.

When studying things like pollution or disease in science class, you can examine if groups of people are affected more than others. Look into the reasons why that is the case, then think about creating informational material to reduce risks.

Computers and the Internet are magnificent tools for researching and creating surveys or brochures for your service-learning projects, but the digital world itself can be the subject as well.

Computer classes are fantastic for creating surveys or databases to collect ideas about positive changes to the community and making them accessible. Technology is also good for connecting those who are willing to provide a service to those who are in need. In an age in which use of the Internet is becoming increasingly indispensible in everyday life, it would also make for a good service-learning project to create a training course for those who don't have access to it, such as the elderly. A course in how to navigate the Internet safely would also benefit many community members. Cyberbullying is a worthy subject as well. The more time we spend online, the more important the question of how we treat each other in this medium becomes.

Physical education classes can be a place to address matters of social justice as well, as long as they are not restricted to playing sports and are concerned with health. You can look into whether all members of your community have access to sports facilities, how poverty affects nutrition, and what effects intercultural games and sports can have.

This list is far from conclusive, but it should make clear that there are many different ways to address community needs. These methods use many different skills, allowing ample opportunity for those willing to work toward social change to make an impact.

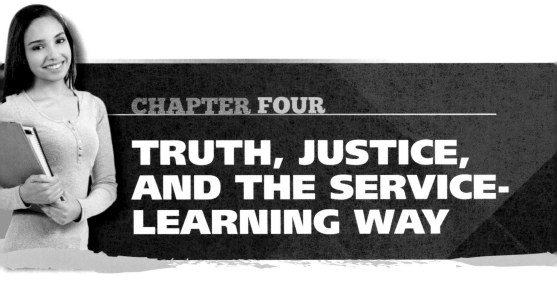

CHAPTER FOUR

TRUTH, JUSTICE, AND THE SERVICE-LEARNING WAY

While service-learning projects can be viewed through the lens of the four categories of service discussed earlier (direct service, indirect service, advocacy, and research) there are also other ways to categorize them. In her book, *Service-Learning and Social Justice*, Susan Benigni Cipolle uses categories that are similar but focus more on what she calls the "ethic of service." She identifies three stages of this ethic of service, which, in ascending order, are charity, caring, and social justice. A proverb is used to explain these different stages: "Give a man a fish and you feed him for a day; teach a man to fish and you feed him for a lifetime." Giving a man a fish is charity, a short-term solution to the problem where there is a clear hierarchy between the person who gives and the person who takes. Teaching a man to fish falls into the category of caring, giving someone the opportunity to not have to rely on charity. The recipient and the service provider are on more equal footing, but they are not the same yet. That stage would be social justice. Cipolle adds an addendum to the proverb for this category of her ethic of service: "Make room at the river for all to fish."

These categories are not necessarily mutually exclusive in a service-learning project. Teaching a man to fish might be easier and a more agreeable experience for all involved if he doesn't have to learn on an empty stomach. Making room at the river for all to fish is not something that is likely to happen overnight, so addressing immediate needs is still a concern.

However, the three stages of this ethic of service go hand in hand with a person's understanding of society. They form a hierarchy with social change at the top and charity on the bottom.

WHAT'S WRONG WITH CHARITY?

In and of itself, nothing is wrong with charity. Charity is, of course, positive. Giving to those in need is better than not doing it. In Cipolle's ethic of service, charity does not simply denote the act of giving, but rather the state of mind of the person being charitable.

The motivation of those being charitable needs to be considered, as some don't do it out of the goodness of their hearts, but rather because they consider it to be an obligation or because it benefits them. This may be because it makes them feel good or because it looks good on college or job applications. The service of those who are inclined to say that they get back more than they give through their charitable activities seems selfish rather than selfless. Feeling good about the service you are providing can and should be a welcome side effect to charity. It should not be the main goal, though.

While it is probably better to be charitable for the wrong reasons than not to be charitable at all, it is not likely for that kind of service to lead to social change. After all, it perpetuates a mentality that pits those who

Being charitable and meeting the immediate needs of others is good, but it can only be the first step on the way to social justice.

give charity against those who receive it. Even though the recipients get something out of charity given with questionable motivations, it can be argued that they are being exploited by somebody who does not truly care about them, is indifferent toward them, and may even secretly loathe them. People pick up on this, and it is not uncommon for people to go hungry (or having another need unfulfilled) rather than having their pride hurt.

With more information about and experience with those receiving charity, the people serving them will likely enter a second stage that elevates them beyond doing charity mainly for themselves: the stage of caring. More exposure to the recipients of charity will help volunteers develop compassion as they realize that the people in need of charity are individuals, not stereotypes. Being able to compare and contrast their stories with your own life can be enlightening and lead to a greater awareness of yourself, others, and the way privilege works in society. Recipients of charity are often described as "less fortunate." But was it really fortune that led to their situation, or was it the underlying power relations at work in society? Members of the middle and upper classes often don't venture out of their social circles, which are comprised largely of other members of the same class. The problems of the lower classes or minorities may be something they have no firsthand experience with and are only aware of because they read about them or saw them on the news. The personal stories of individuals, which may well contain examples of biases and injustices they suffered, can have a much greater impact and lead to the final stage of the hierarchy, the desire to change the

Getting to know people from different backgrounds and walks of life will help you understand the challenges they face and maybe give you a new perspective on social justice.

system that allows for these biases and injustices, level the playing field, and bring about social change.

THINKING IS CRITICAL

To be able to address social issues, you first have to be aware of them. Things like intolerance and discrimination obviously exist, and you don't need to experience them yourself to be able to perceive inequality in regard to rights, status, and wealth. But rather than seeing these as problems of society as a whole, some people place the sole responsibility with the individual. They are of the opinion that those in need have only themselves to blame, that if they simply worked harder, they would not be in a position in which they need charity or support from others. When you are dealing with the topics

When engaged in a service-learning project concerned with social justice, it is important to think critically about what you think you know about society.

of tolerance and social change, though, you need to ask yourself if that is true. The Declaration of Independence may state that all men are created equal, but that does not mean that everybody has the same opportunities in life. If somebody is constantly met with prejudice and discrimination because of who they are, be it the color of their skin, their gender, or their sexual preference, it is naive to think that everybody is basically the same and some are just less fortunate than others. There are social barriers that hinder some groups within society. If you want to tear barriers down, you first have to be able to identify them.

Some people claim that they do not see differences between people. It is particularly common for people to claim they are "colorblind," or do not register differences in race. While the hearts of these people may be in the right place (provided they're not simply saying what they think is expected of them) in that they want to express that to them all people are equal, they are trying to ignore a problem rather than face and solve it. Of course the differences themselves are not the problem; they are something to be valued, as they are part of what makes people who they are. Claiming to not see an integral part of a person means robbing that person of her individuality and not accepting her for who she is. Even if one person saw all people as equal, that does not mean society as a whole does. Biases and prejudices still play a part in everyday life, and that is a factor that needs to be recognized.

To this end, every responsible member of society has to develop what Brazilian educator and philosopher

❯ AFFIRMATIVE ACTION

Affirmative action tries to level the playing field. Through affirmative action, women and members of minority groups get easier admission to institutions of higher education and better employment opportunities. This measure is deemed necessary to compensate for the discrimination members of these groups have suffered for a long time.

Affirmative action policies were first introduced to benefit African Americans under President Lyndon B. Johnson. He argued in his commencement address at Howard University on June 4, 1965: "You do not take a person who, for years, has been hobbled by chains and liberate him, bring him up to the starting line of a race and then say, 'You are free to compete with all the others,' and still justly believe that you have been completely fair. Thus it is not enough just to open the gates of opportunity. All our citizens must have the ability to walk through those gates."

Affirmative action based on other criteria (such as disability, gender, or age) was introduced later on. These policies were and still are a controversial topic, as they are seen by some as a form of reverse discrimination directed at those who are not part of a minority and usually not victims of discrimination. Therefore, affirmative action has been the subject of numerous court cases since the 1970s.

Paulo Freire (1921–1997) called a critical consciousness. "Critical" here does not mean to criticize something in a negative way. Instead it is a way of looking at something and not accepting it at face value. Critically conscious people will think for themselves rather than accept uncritically what they are told. They will examine if what they are told has merit. Therefore those who think critically are less susceptible to prejudices.

The word "prejudice" comes from the Latin *praeiudicium*. *Prae* means "before," while *iudicium* means "judgement." So a prejudice is a judgement made before the actual evidence is considered, based on a preconceived opinion that can derive from past personal experiences but is often adopted from others like family members and friends, taking their word for it rather than forming an opinion of their own. Some biases are ingrained very deeply in our society, forming an accepted view of the world, a set of ideas

Paulo Freire, who first devised critical pedagogy, wanted to help students develop the ability to look beneath the surface and understand how society works.

and norms that is so powerful that it can prevent other ideas from even being considered, since it is constantly reinforced through the media and institutions we are in contact with every day. This seemingly commonsensical understanding of how the world works and how it has to work is referred to as "hegemony." The word comes from the Greek and means "dominance," particularly a dominance of one group of people over others that is cemented through an accepted view of the world that makes it difficult to even imagine the world could function in a different way.

The commonly held view is that the United States is the embodiment of the ideals of freedom and justice, a place where everybody has an equal chance at success and happiness. Somebody with a critical consciousness will not simply accept this claim as a fact but will judge for himself or herself. That person will ask who benefits from and who is handicapped by the way things are.

Questioning one's own beliefs and identifying one's own prejudices can be difficult and even painful. Still, it is worthwhile to be intellectually independent and to see things for what they are rather than for what others tell you they are. Service learning aims to help students become valuable members of their communities, able to identify and address community needs. Being able to think critically and freely is the most important tool for that.

CHAPTER FIVE

EXAMPLES OF SERVICE LEARNING IN ACTION

The possibilities for service learning are almost endless. There are countless ideas that either have been turned into a project already or are still waiting to be put into practice. Some of the best ideas come from looking at the needs of one's own community. These problems may require unconventional and unique solutions. It can't hurt to take a look at what others have done, though, to see what is possible and maybe draw some inspiration from it.

UGANDA GOT MAIL

A powerful example of how service learning can lead to a greater awareness of others and prompt participants to think about their own privilege is the Postcards to Africa project started by associate professor Belle Liang at Boston College in 2008. The project connected students in the United States to teenagers in Uganda through postcards they exchanged. The project expanded so that it included middle school students as well as students from Boston College. The students wrote to youths in the war-torn African country to tell them about their lives. In return, they learned about the lives of their pen pals, which in many cases had been affected by the conflict in their home country. While one might expect that having a pen pal from overseas might mean little to a teenager who has been orphaned or was drafted as a child soldier, Liang notes, in a story in the *Boston College Chronicle*, "Exchanging postcards . . . would hardly seem to make a difference, until you realize few if any of these children have ever received or sent a piece of mail in their lives. Getting letters from some-one increases these children's sense of connection with the world, so they feel less isolated. It tells them another young person out there wants to know them and cares about them, which is a tremendous boost to their self-worth and well-being."

> WORKING TOGETHER OR ACTING ALONE

Many service-learning projects that offer direct or indirect service cooperate with local institutions like shelters or food banks. Projects that have social change as their goal also have the option of working together with established national or international organizations. As these probably have a broader scope and may not have an office in your area, there are a few things to consider. While you can see for yourself if a local institution works in accordance with your ideas, you will have to investigate nonlocal institutions in another way. Most will have websites where you can read their mission statements and see examples of what they do so that you know whether or not they have the same goals as you. Looking up how an organization presents itself should only be a starting point, though. To verify their claims, you can look them up on websites like the Exempt Organizations Select Check provided by the IRS (www.irs.gov/Charities-&-Non-Profits/Exempt-Organizations-Select-Check) or GuideStar (www.guidestar.org), a charity that presents information on registered nonprofit organizations for the sake of transparency.

Checking the goals and the legitimacy of an organization is one thing, but you also need to ask yourself if a collaboration is truly beneficial, not only for your service-learning project but for the organization as well. If the staff of an established organization has to spend more time instructing students than they save through the students' contributions, the common cause both share may not be best served. On the other hand, the cause may benefit in the long run by organizations helping students become leaders in their own communities. Since service-learning projects in schools usually only last a few weeks, it might be best to consider collaborations for projects that can be finished in a limited amount of time but will benefit the organization (and thus the cause) continuously. One example would be putting together or translating brochures. Since many schools offer service-learning projects every year, it may also be possible to establish a prolonged collaboration, although individual students will naturally be part of it for only a short time.

For the students in the United States, some of whom continued to correspond with the Ugandan students after the service-learning project had ended, the experience was humbling. The effects of war and poverty on young people became clearer and more personal. The cross-cultural exchange offered a fresh perspective on both sides.

THE WRITING ON THE WALL

After discussing homophobic name-calling, the service-learning class at Highland Park Junior High in Saint Paul, Minnesota, wanted to promote their school as safe for gay, lesbian, bisexual, and transgender students and staff, addressing a need in their immediate community. To this end, they interviewed students who were "out" as homosexual about their struggles in school and came up with a plan to create a mural. When the principal rejected the idea, they were disappointed. Then their teacher encouraged them to find out why he had said no. The reason was not that he thought the idea too controversial, as they had suspected. He supported their goal, but was worried that the terms used in the mural might become outdated after a few years. This is not an unfounded concern when you consider how the terminology used by the LGBTQ community has changed over the past three decades (with the "T," for transgender, and the "Q," for queer or questioning, being fairly recent additions). Instead of giving up on their idea, the students adjusted it to the concerns of their principal. Rather than painting a permanent mural, they created a bannerlike quilt out of colorful fabric that got the message across just as well but was more versatile as it could be (and was) hung in different parts of the school. To further advocate the issue, parts of the students' design were incorporated into a poster and a brochure used by the Saint Paul Public School District's program Out for Equity, which pursues the goal of a safe and welcoming school environment for LGBTQ students, staff members, and families.

When faced with an obstacle in the pursuit of a service-learning endeavor, it is important to not simply give up. Instead consider the problem from different perspectives and try to find a solution. It may turn out even better than the original plan!

Teachers or principals sometimes have to restrict the ideas their students come up with. Discussing the reasons for that, you can usually find a solution that is satisfactory for all involved.

ANIMAL RIGHTS ADVOCACY

Human behavior does not only affect other humans. Our lifestyle has consequences for the other living beings we share planet Earth with, a fact students from Crane Country Day School in Santa Barbara, California, drew attention to in a "We Speak for the Animals" fair at which they collected donations for the World Wildlife

When looking at injustices in society, the treatment of animals is a concern that can be addressed through service learning.

Fund. The fair took place on Earth Day, an annual global holiday on which two hundred countries to promote a more environment-conscious way of living.

Thirty students from kindergarten through eighth grade participated in the fair, which was not required but done independently by the students. Given the opportunity to create a service-learning program about a topic they cared about personally, students were happy to inform others about animal cruelty as well as endangered species like leopards and koalas. Students discussed the reasons why these animals are in danger of extinction. Usually humans are to blame because they hunt the animals or destroy their natural habitat. Only a change in our lifestyle will give endangered animals a chance to survive. This kind of sweeping change in human lifestyles would require major social change. Seventh-grade student Forest Dempsey, one of the founder's of Crane's first animal rights clubs, explained in an article that Ann Pieramici wrote for Noozhawk.com, "We really wanted to educate people because the animals can't speak for themselves," making this a prime example for advocacy in a service learning project.

HONORING SACRIFICES BY MAKING AN EXAMPLE

Hundreds of members of the Kentucky National Guard have perished while serving their fellow citizens, a sacrifice that has not been honored enough. To change that, the construction of a memorial is planned at the

Members of the Kentucky National Guard, seen here landing in Tucson, Arizona, have made great sacrifices serving their fellow citizens.

entrance to Boone National Guard Center in Frankfort, Kentucky. Students from King Middle School in Mercer County, Kentucky, showed their support by designing and selling T-shirts. They raised $5,000 for the memorial in the fall of 2013, learning about the sacrifices of the citizen soldiers in the National Guard as well as economic decisions. While $5,000 is a lot of money, it is only a small part of the estimated $1.4 million needed for the memorial. But the school did not stop there. Spearheading the fund-raising effort, King Middle School promoted the cause and encouraged other schools to participate by collecting loose change and donating these "Pennies for Honor" to the memorial fund. The school's effort made an impact by drawing attention to the issue of how the community treated its veterans, prompting businesses and organizations to donate to the memorial fund. Joshua Witt, volunteer coordinator on the memorial, called the school's initial donation the catalyst after which the fund-raising took off exponentially. As seventh-grade student Mckenzie Dunbar told Kendra Peek of the *Advocate Messenger*, "When we raised $5,000 . . . that set off a chain reaction that others said that if a middle school can do it, we can do it, too." A small contribution can have great—monumental, even—effect, a valuable lesson in service learning and addressing a community need.

Its organizers hope that the Kentucky National Guard Memorial becomes a popular destination for field trips, giving many more students the opportunity to learn about the history of the National Guard.

SERVICE LEARNING WITH SUPERPOWERS

The Comic Book Project gives students the opportunity to create comics of their own, raising awareness of issues important to them. Founded by Michael Bitz as an after-school program in an elementary school in New York City, the project has expanded quickly since its start in 2001 and has seen successful projects launched all over the United States and even internationally, with new programs established in Canada, Mexico, and Nicaragua. Students of all ages get to be creative and practice their writing, work in a medium they enjoy, and get a glimpse into what many consider a dream job. The most successful books are printed by Dark Horse Comics and distributed in schools for free. Covering topics like bullying and conflict resolution, drug abuse, environmental awareness, racism, financial education, or the life stories of migrant youths, the books created through this project can be very informative and educational for their readers. Teachers who have often denounced comics as an inferior form of literature are discovering that they make a great learning tool, one that can be used to advocate issues of social change.

SO MANY OPTIONS

If you're interested in finding more examples of service-learning projects, there are many ways to start your search. If your school has a service-learning program, you could ask the staff members who coordinate it or the kids who took part in it in previous years which programs were the most successful. The websites of groups such as the National Youth Leadership Council and GenerationOn offer profiles of projects. The National Service-Learning Clearinghouse website

There are countless ideas for service-learning projects to be found on the Internet, which you can use as inspiration to get involved yourself.

(http://gsn.nylc.org/clearinghouse) lets you both look for projects and connect to people working on them. There are plenty of ideas out there that can help you shape your own plans for a project that can make society more tolerant, while also providing an important educational experience for you and your fellow project participants.

GLOSSARY

advocacy A form of service that helps address the root causes of a problem by raising awareness of the issue.

caring Showing empathy and compassion, which turns serving into a mutual relationship.

charity An act of kindness or generosity, like donating money or giving something to eat to the hungry.

civic responsibility The duty a member of a community has to maintain and improve the well-being of said community.

community A town or neighborhood; any group of people that is connected in a way, be it their location or common interests and ideals.

community service Volunteering to serve the community, which is distinct from service learning because of a lack of educational focus and reflection.

critical consciousness A more accurate understanding of the world that does not accept things at face value but considers the underlying causes of social issues.

direct service A form of service in which the one serving and the recipient of the service interact in person.

experiential education An educational philosophy that argues that people learn best from experience and reflecting on that experience.

hegemony The dominance of one group over another, and the view of how the world functions that supports this dominance.

indirect service A form of service in which the one who provides it and the people who benefit from it do not interact in person. Instead of specific individuals, indirect service may benefit the community or the environment as a whole.

pedagogic Having to do with teachers or education.

reflection The act of thinking back on an experience and considering the effect it had.

service A helpful act that addresses a community need.

service learning A teaching method that combines service and learning to address a need, giving students the chance to make a difference in their communities.

social change A change in the way a society works.

social justice A state in which all members of a society have equal rights and equal opportunities to realize their potential.

solidarity A feeling of unity between people who have the same interests or goals.

tolerance The willingness to accept those who are different from yourself for who they are.

FOR MORE INFORMATION

America's Promise Alliance
1110 Vermont Avenue NW, Suite 900
Washington, DC 20005
(202) 657-0600
Website: http://www.americaspromise.org
This partnership strives to create the conditions for all
of America's young people to succeed. It believes
that America must keep five promises to its children
and teens, providing them with caring adults, safe
places, a healthy start, an effective education, and
opportunities to serve.

Canadian Alliance for Community Service-Learning
2128 Dunton Tower
Carleton University
1125 Colonel By Drive
Ottawa, ON K1S 5B6
Canada
(613) 520-2600 x8241
Website: www.communityservicelearning.ca
The Canadian Alliance for Community Service-Learning
aims to educate about and advocate the use of
service learning in Canada by informing students
and educators, creating networks, providing resources, and supporting research.

Canadian CED Network – Réseau canadien de DÉC
59, rue Monfette, P.O. Box 119E
Victoriaville, QC G6P 1J8
Canada
(877) 202-2268
Website: http://ccednet-rcdec.ca/en

This group focuses on community economic development (CED), or efforts by local people to bring about
social change by creating economic opportunities,
especially for disadvantaged communities. Along with
the Storytellers' Foundation, the Canadian CED Network has set up the Community Development Service
Learning (CDSL) Initiative.

GenerationOn
281 Park Avenue South, 6th Floor
New York, NY 10010
(917) 746-8182
Website: http://www.generationon.org
This global youth service organization started out as
a New York City nonprofit group called Children for
Children. In 2009, Children for Children merged
with several other youth service organizations to
become GenerationOn, the youth wing of the Points
of Light service organization.

KIDS Consortium
1300 Old County Road
Waldoboro, ME 04572
(207) 620-8272
Website: www.kidsconsortium.org
KIDS (Kids Involved Doing Service-Learning)
Consortium is a nonprofit organization founded in
1992 that helps schools and communities in New
England and beyond implement service learning and
address community needs.

*Michigan Journal of Community Service
Learning* (MJCSL)

Ginsberg Center, The University of Michigan
1024 Hill Street
Ann Arbor, MI 48104
(734) 763-3548
Website: http://ginsberg.umich.edu/mjcsl
MJCSL is a national, peer-reviewed journal that has
    published research and theoretical articles on
    service learning in higher education since 1994.
    Articles from issues that are over a year old can be
    read for free on the journal's website.

National Service-Learning Clearinghouse
c/o ETR Associates
4 Carbonero Way
Scotts Valley, CA 95066
(800) 860-2684
Website: http://gsn.nylc.org
This organization's website is a great way to
    get more information about service-learning
    programs throughout the United States. It lets
    users search for programs, share planning ideas,
    and discuss their projects with others, and offers
    an array of service-learning professional develop-
    ment resources.

National Society for Experiential Education (NSEE)
19 Mantua Road
Mount Royal, NJ 08061
(856) 423-3427
Website: http://www.nsee.org
Founded in 1971, the National Society for Experien-
    tial Education is made up of a mix of educators,

businesses, and community leaders. It is a re-
source center for experiential education programs
across the United States.

National Youth Leadership Council (NYLC)
1667 Snelling Avenue North, Suite D300
Saint Paul, MN 55108
(651) 631-3672
Website: http://www.nylc.org
Established in 1983, NYLC has been following its
   mission to empower youth and create a more just
   world through service learning for more than thirty
   years. On NYLC's website you can find the National
   Service-Learning Clearinghouse (http://gsn.nylc
   .org/clearinghouse), an online library offering
   thousands of free service-learning resources.

Rethinking Schools
1001 East Keefe Avenue
Milwaukee, WI 53212
(414) 964-9646
Website: http://www.rethinkingschools.org
A nonprofit publisher and advocacy organization with
   almost thirty years of history, Rethinking Schools is
   committed to the idea that public education is cen-
   tral to the creation of a humane, caring, multiracial
   democracy. Its resources for teachers, parents, and
   students promote equity and racial justice in the
   classroom.

Youth for Human Rights
1920 Hillhurst Avenue, #416

Los Angeles, CA 90027
(323) 663-5799
Website: http://www.youthforhumanrights.org
Founded in 2001, this nonprofit organization aims to
teach young people about human rights and inspire
them to become advocates for tolerance and peace
both in the classroom and less traditional settings.

Youth Service America (YSA)
1101 15th Street, NW, Suite 200
Washington, DC 20005
(202) 296-2992
Website: http://www.ysa.org
Youth Service America aims to increase the number
and diversity of young people serving their communities through grants, training, and resources,
as well as large-scale campaigns like Global Youth
Service Day.

WEBSITES

Because of the changing nature of Internet links,
Rosen Publishing has developed an online list of
websites related to the subject of this book. This site is
updated regularly. Please use this link to access this list:

http://www.rosenlinks.com/SLFT/Tole

FOR FURTHER READING

Baca, Isabel, ed. *Service-Learning and Writing: Paving the Way for Literacy(ies) Through Community Engagement*. Boston, MA: Brill, 2012.

Birkenmaier, Julie, Ashley Cruce, Jan Wilson, Jami Curley, Ellen Burkemper, and John Stretch, eds. *Educating for Social Justice: Transformative Experiential Learning*. Chicago, IL: Lyceum Books, 2011.

Bringle, Robert G., Julie A. Hatcher, and Steven G. Jones, eds. *International Service Learning: Conceptual Frameworks and Research*. Sterling, VA: Stylus, 2011.

Cooksey, M. A., and Kimberley T. Olivares, eds. *Quick Hits for Service-Learning: Successful Strategies by Award-Winning Teachers*. Bloomington, IN: Indiana University Press, 2010.

Cress, Christine Marie. *Learning Through Serving: A Student Guidebook for Service-Learning and Civic Engagement Across Academic Disciplines and Cultural Communities*. 2nd Ed. Sterlina, VA: Stylus Publshing, 2013.

Dutkiewicz, Piotr, and Richard Sakwa, eds. *22 Ideas to Fix the World: Conversations with the World's Foremost Thinkers*. New York, NY: New York University Press, 2013.

Farber, Katy. *Change the World with Service Learning: How to Organize, Lead, and Assess Service Learning Projects*. Lanham, MD: Rowman & Littlefield Education, 2011.

Friedman, Janey, and Jolene Roehlkepartain. *Doing Good Together: 101 Easy, Meaningful Service Projects for Families, Schools, and Communities*. Minneapolis, MN: Free Spirit Publishing, 2010.

Hatcher, Julia A., and Robert G. Bringle, eds. *Understanding Service-Learning and Community Engagement: Making Engaged Scholarship Matter*. Charlotte, NC: Information Age Publishing, 2012.

Henslin, James M. *Social Problems: A Down-to-Earth Approach*. 11th ed. Boston, MA: Pearson, 2014.

Hobert, Carl. *Raising Global IQ: Preparing Our Students for a Shrinking Planet*. Boston, MA: Beacon Press, 2013.

Lewis, Barbara A. *The Kid's Guide to Service Projects: Over 500 Service Ideas for Young People Who Want to Make a Difference*. Updated 2nd ed. Minneapolis, MN: Free Spirit Publishing, 2009.

Lewis, Barbara A. *The Teen Guide to Global Action: How to Connect with Others (Near & Far) to Create Social Change*. Minneapolis, MN: Free Spirit Publishing, 2008.

Kapin, Allyson, and Amy Sample Ward. *Social Change Anytime Anywhere: How to Implement Online Multichannel Strategies to Spark Advocacy, Raise Money, and Engage Your Community*. San Francisco, CA: Jossey-Bass, 2013.

Murphy, Timothy, and Jon Tan, eds. *Service-Learning and Educating in Challenging Contexts: International Perspectives*. New York, NY: Continuum, 2012.

O'Neal, Claire. *Volunteering in Your School*. Hockessin, DE: Mitchell Lane Publishers, 2011.

Purmensky, Kerry L. *Service-Learning for Diverse Communities: Critical Pedagogy and Mentoring English Language Learners*. Charlotte, NC: Information Age Publishing, 2009.

Stenhouse, Vera L., Olga S. Jarrett, Rhina M. Fernandes Williams, and Elizabeth Namisi Chilungu.

In the Service of Learning and Empowerment: Service-Learning, Critical Pedagogy, and the Problem-Solution Project. Charlotte, NC: Information Age Publishing, 2014.

Stoecker, Randy, and Elizabeth A. Tryon, eds. *The Unheard Voices: Community Organizations and Service Learning*. Philadelphia, PA: Temple University Press, 2009.

Strait, Jean, and Marybeth Lima, eds. *The Future of Service-Learning: New Solutions for Sustaining and Improving Practice*. Sterling, VA: Stylus 2009.

Westover, Jonathan H. *Academic Service-Learning Across Disciplines: Models, Outcomes, and Assessment*. Champaign, IL: Common Ground Publishing, 2012.

BIBLIOGRAPHY

Cipolle, Susan Benigni. *Service-Learning and Social Justice: Engaging Students in Social Change.* Lanham, MD: Rowman & Littlefield Publishers, 2010.

Habib, Deborah Leta. *Schools Serving for Social Justice: Stories of Inspiration, Strategies for Implementation.* Washington, DC: Corporation for National Service, 2000. Retrieved May 14, 2014 (https://www.national serviceresources.gov/files/legacy/filemanager/down load/NatlServFellows/habib1.pdf).

Johnson, Lyndon B. "Commencement Address at Howard University: 'To Fulfill These Rights,' June 4, 1965." Retrieved May 9, 2014 (http://www.lbjlib. utexas.edu/johnson/archives.hom/speeches. hom/650604.asp).

Kaye, Cathryn Berger. *The Complete Guide to Service Learning: Proven, Practical Ways to Engage Students in Civic Responsibility, Academic Curriculum, & Social Action.* 2nd ed. Minneapolis, MN: Free Spirit Publishing, 2010.

Morton, Keith. "The Irony of Service: Charity, Project and Social Chance in Service-Learning." *Michigan Journal of Community and Service Learning*, Volume 2, Issue 1, 1995. Retrieved May 1, 2014 (http://quod.lib.umich.edu/m/ mjcsl/3239521.0002.102/1).

Morton, Keith, and John Saltmarsh. "Addams, Day, and Dewey: The Emergence of Community Service in American Culture." *Michigan Journal of Community and Service Learning*, Volume 4, Issue 1, 1997. Retrieved March 26, 2014 (http://quod.lib.umich. edu/m/mjcsl/3239521.0004.117/1).

Peek, Kendra. "Mercer Students Take Active Role

Fundraising to Honor Guard Members." *The Advocate Messenger*, April 7, 2014. Retrieved May 13, 2014 (http://www.centralkynews.com/amnews/news/local/mercer/mercer-students-take-active-role-fundraising-to-honor-guard-members/article_5950837e-3370-5ad6-9fa7-a5e008b5a6c9.html).

Pieramici, Ann. "Crane Students Speak for the Animals on Earth Day." Noozhawk.com, April 29, 2014. Retrieved May 13, 2014 (http://www.noozhawk.com/article/crane_students_speak_for_the_animals_on_earth_day_20140429).

Rautio, Ann. *Service-Learning in the United States: Status of Institutionalization*. Denver, CO: Education Commission of the States, 2012. Retrieved April 11, 2014 (http://ncasl.org/articulate/policy/data/downloads/10155.pdf).

Riddell, Susan. "Mercer Co. Middle School Students Tackle a Monumental Service Learning Project." KyForward.com, April 21, 2014. Retrieved May 13, 2014 (http://www.kyforward.com/our-schools/2014/04/21/mercer-co-middle-school-students-tackle-a-monumental-service-learning-project).

Ryan, Molly. *Service-Learning After Learn and Serve America: How Five States Are Moving Forward*. Denver, CO: Education Commission of the States, 2012. Retrieved April 11, 2014 (http://www.nylc.org/sites/nylc.org/files/09-ECS%20NCLC%20Report%20-%20Service-Learning%20After%20LSA.pdf).

Seifert, Anne, Sandra Zentner, and Franziska Nagy. *Praxisbuch Service-Learning. "Lernen durch Engagement" an Schulen*. Weinheim, Germany: Beltz Verlag, 2012.

Smith, Sean. "Postcards Deliver Hope. New LSOE Program Reaches Out to Troubled Ugandan Children." *Boston College Chronicle*, June 24, 2008. Retrieved May 14, 2014 (http://www.bc.edu/publications/chronicle/TopstoriesNewFeatures/features/postcards031209.html).

Speck, Bruce W., and Sherry Lee Hoppe, eds. *Service-Learning: History, Theory, and Issues*. Westport, CT: Praeger Publishers, 2004.

Strauss, Valerie. "Thinking Outside the Box, Inside the Panel." *Washington Post*, June 15, 2004. Retrieved May 14, 2014 (http://www.washingtonpost.com/wp-dyn/articles/A41684-2004Jun14.html).

Titlebaum, Peter, Gabrielle Williamson, Corinne Daprano, Janine Baer, and Jayne Brahler. "Annotated History of Service Learning 1862–2002." April 11, 2014. Retrieved May 14, 2014 (http://www.fsu.edu/~flserve/resources/resource%20files/annotated%20history.pdf).

Wilczenski, Felicia L., and Susan M. Commey. *A Practical Guide to Service Learning: Strategies for Positive Development in Schools*. New York, NY: Springer Science+Business Media, 2007.

Youth Dreamers. "About Us: Our History." Retrieved April 18, 2014 (http://www.youthdreamers.org/pages/aboutus.htm).

INDEX

ABOUT THE AUTHOR

Dr. Nicki Peter Petrikowski is a literary scholar as well as an editor, author, and translator. He was first introduced to the concept of service learning at the ripe old age of nine, raising awareness of the consequences of the volcanic activity of Mount Pinatubo while in elementary school.

PHOTO CREDITS

Cover Kevork Djansezian/Getty Images; p. 3 bymandesigns/Shutterstock .com; pp. 4–5 Blend Images/KidStock/Brand X Pictures/Getty Images; p. 7 FuzzBones/Shutterstock.com; pp. 8, 41, 45 Monkey Business Images/Shutterstock.com; p. 10 Fuse/Thinkstock; p. 13 SuperStock/Getty Images; pp. 16–17 Steve Debenport/E+/Getty Images; p. 18 Courtesy Cheyenne River Youth Project/AP Images; p. 19 © iStockphoto. com/eurobanks p. 20 mangostock/Shutterstock.com; p. 23 Alexander Raths/Shutterstock.com; p. 26 Yellow Dog Productions/The Image Bank/ Getty Images; pp. 28–29 Goodluz/Shutterstock.com; p. 30 Blend Images/ Hill Street Studios/Brand X Pictures/Getty Images; p. 32 Flashon Studio/ Shutterstock.com; p. 33 Library of Congress Prints and Photographs Division; pp. 36–37 Dragon Images/Shutterstock.com; p. 38 Simone Becchetti/Vetta/Getty Images; p. 43 Antonio Guillem/Shutterstock.com; p. 47 Purestock/Getty Images; p. 48 KPG Payless/Shutterstock.com; p. 51 Globo/Getty Images; p. 53 Tom Wang/Shutterstock.com; p. 57 Keith Brofsky/UpperCut Images/Getty Images; p. 58 pojoslaw/iStock/Thinkstock; p. 60 Gary Williams/Getty Images; p. 63 ASchindl/Shutterstock.com; cover and interior pages background textures and patterns vector illustration/ Shutterstock.com, Apostrophe/Shutterstock.com, nattanan726/ Shutterstock.com, Yulia Glam/Shutterstock.com; back cover silhouette Pavel L Photo and Video/Shutterstock.com.

Designer: Michael Moy; Editor: Jeanne Nagle